Magic Mirrors

Divination, Clairvoyance, Astral Kingdoms, Evocation, Consecrations, the Urim and Thummim, Mirrors of the Bhattahs, Arabs, Nostradamus, Swedenborg, Cagliostro

By Paul Sédir

1907 3rd edition

Translated by Alex Bushman 2019

Contents

Introduction

At no time has man been satisfied with the wonders of the physical world; from the beginning of societies he had the intuition of an beyond and an invisible, the desire of the infinite; a miserable and lonely creature struggling incessantly against formidable fate, he instinctively sought in himself a logic to guide his march, a light to encourage his untiring hope. I will not repeat the development, easy to describe, of primitive societies, or rudimentary cults; the readers know this way of the cross of humanity, at all stages of which the physical wound has bloomed a new spiritual flower.

Divination arose from the cries of anguish and questioning which our pitiful ancestor uttered to the loud voice of the waters, to the song of the forests, to the stars; the bird hovering in the heavens, the animal encountered on the road, the meteor illuminating the night, gave answers to his unspoken requests; Physical Nature, therefore, contributed first to the edification of this great science of omens.

But, if we refer to the sources of the occult tradition, we will learn that angelic entities were always committed by the Supreme Wisdom to the direction of the triple evolutionary movement of the planet: some of these angels failed; the cohort of Adepts contains the mystic threads of both camps. Through them innumerable and scattered notions were united in a system of science, and their mental theories, assented with perfect completeness, always identified themselves with archetypal laws.

The principal of these laws, and the most fundamental at the same time as the most important, is that of the Trinity[1].

I will try to apply it here to the vast system of Divination.

Man is triple: Body, doubly polarized soul, spirit[2].

The Cosmos is triple: Natura naturata, Humanity (Adam of Genesis), Natura Naturans (spirits, planetary geniuses, angels). Placed in the center of the Cosmos, Man can therefore interrogate each of his three parts specially, according to one or other of his three faculties: this is the basis of our classification.

The physical Man questions the body of Nature; hence divination is born by natural omens; that he questions other men, the soul of Nature, he will create all the parts of the physiognomy; that he questions the spirits, they will answer him around the magic circle.

The animistic Man will find the answers of nature in the images of dreams; he will be able to read in the souls of other men by developing his spiritual senses; and he will hear the spirits speak to him, in the sacred sleep of ecstasy. If at last it is the spirit that is anxious and worried, the sky will answer it by the deductions of astrology, the magic chain of the human initiation will make speak the tarot, the ancient teraphim, or even the Light of the Word will inspire him with conscious prophecies. The following table will better capture these classifications.

---

[1] Regarding the Trinity, refer to the admirable works of Lacuria and Barlet.
[2] Papus: *Treatise of Practical Magic,* 1906 and *Sciences of the Mages*

		ADAM		
The Cosmos	The Non-Ego	Physical Man	Astral Man	Intellectual Man
	Natura Naturata	Natural Omens	Dreams	Judicial Astrology
	Humanity	General Physiognomy	Astral Sensitivity (clairvoyance, etc.)	Tarot
	Natura Naturans	Magic (physical manifestations of the invisible)	Ecstasy	Conscious Prophecy

We see from the very first glance that by virtue of the very principle of Yoga, one who wants to possess the control of divination will first have to ensure that his astral development (box 5 in the table) is the center of the whole system, the solar point of all culture.

The magic mirror is none other than the instrument of the esoteric culture of the astral senses. We can judge its importance by that. I will add, however, that such a subject is beyond my strength, and that I have no intention of exhausting it in the following pages. A simple preliminary elucidation of the hyperphysics in man and outside man, with the means of penetrating the densest regions, this is the plan of this study.

Whatever the imperfections may be, I shall consider myself happy if the sincere workers can withdraw some useful information from this reading.

However, I must add here that this little book is somehow second best. I do not advise anyone to practice magic under any of its forms. To give the reasons for this would require an entire volume; nevertheless, I have written these pages to give the least dangerous method of voluntarily going into the astral, so that people in a hurry can satisfy their curiosity without running any physical risks. They will face other obstacles; but these will be in over a longer term than the previous ones.

Chapter 1: Theory

I.   The Invisible

More than at any other time in Western history, the minds shaped by today's science are embarking on the endless labyrinth of the phenomenal world. Scientists of encyclopedic erudition have succeeded in large numbers to build simple classifications of the same particular sciences: wasted effort; the facts of observation come every day to destroy the best built theories, for want of an elusive link of which very few have known the existence, and of which a still smaller number, among those who knew it, could use it effectively.

This link, a balancing term and a channel between two opposites, the reader has already guessed, is the third term of the Trinity. To the impartial student of ancient religious symbolisms, the Trinity appears as the capital law of creation; indeed, all dogmas proclaim it in first place. This general law must therefore be equally true in its particular applications.

Here we refer the reader to Papus's luminous exposé on the three worlds of the Universe.

"Each organic or inorganic form that manifests itself to our senses is a statuette from a great artist who is called the creator, or rather who comes from a higher plane which we call the plane of creation.

Between this higher plane and our visible physical world, there is an intermediary plane to receive the impressions of the higher plane and to realize them by acting on the matter.[3] "

It is this intermediate plane that the occult tradition calls the *astral plane.*

Since any phenomenon belongs *ipso facto* to the physical world, since its primary cause belongs to the ideal, metaphysical world, the means by which it manifests belongs to the world of laws, to the astral world.

Protected by infinite forms, the astral is that milieu, that universal mediator, which passively receives the positive influences of the principles of the *world*; it nourishes them in its bosom, develops them, organizes them, and has vitalized them, it serves them, becomes an integral part of itself, and its own fertile faculties, to the modeling of the ultimate elevation of matter, of this recently understood protyle[4]. By the effect of the physical forces we know, this second fertilization will develop the visible phenomena, both glory and despair of positive science.

Such is the opinion of Tradition: between a cause and an effect always acts the especially and spontaneously adapted faculty to the double nature of the principle and the goal to be attained[5]. What I have just sketched so roughly is none

---

[3] *La Science des Mages et ses applications*

[4] A.B.: protyle – A hypothetical base substance from which all chemical elements were believed to have been made; subatomic particles.

[5] The faculty of adaptation considered in a general way and in all its forms, is the Fo - Hat of the initiates of the north of India, it is the Sakti, the feminine of the great gods, for the brahmin initiates, it is is Adam, Eve, etc. – Refer to Genesis.

other than the most general quaternary revolution, of which we can see the movement masterfully described in the admirable works of the contemporary masters of occultism.

This, then, is the true nature of this invisible mystery, which frightens us by its depth, and which escapes our research with such versatility as soon as we wish to interrogate it.

Now, does this protean faculty of adaptation, which is the very essence of the astral, since it is manifested by movement, is it life? Is the astral a living being, or a huge community of living individuals? The analogy requires answering in the affirmative. Moreover, the highest initiates, like the most famous exoteric philosophers, have recognized the universe as a whole in perpetual transformation from which death (taken in the strict sense of equilibrium, of nothingness) is excluded[6].

Here we are led to conclude, in agreement with the sages of the most remote times: Like all that moves, all that lives, the Invisible is at once a being and an immense assembly of beings; physical man is the aggregate of innumerable cells, he himself is a cell of the cosmic body of Adam Kadmon. That the gigantic proportions of occult individualities pass our ordinary conceptions, that what appears to us as an unconscious medium is in reality an individual endowed with body, soul and spirit, it is what a deeper meditation will convince us of, it is such a sublime spectacle that the magic mirror can bring us to witness.

There are six of these universal faculties, synthesized in a seventh.
[6] Refer to among others, the *Monadology* of Leibnitz.

Let's recapitulate this somewhat obscure data. Extremely simple principles, infinitely multiple phenomena, between them, channels, organs; thus appears the universe to which it penetrates from the exterior to the interior. To prove this Invisible, or better yet, to put every sincere and well-disposed student on the path that can lead him (if he desires it) to the threshold of the ocean of light and life in which the worlds float; this is the purpose of this essay.

II.   <u>Clairvoyance</u>

Clairvoyance is the faculty of seeing everything beyond the reach of our physical sight. Clairvoyance can be exercised in time or in space. In time, it uncovers future things (forebodings, prophecies, etc.), or it allows one to see things of the past. In space, it produces what psycho -physiologists today call "telepathic visual hallucinations"[7].

Since Mesmer, illustrious philosophers, especially among the Germans, have occupied themselves with this singular faculty of man; they have sought the theory; and it is after Kant, Schopenhauer, after the founder of Monism, Dr. C. du Prel[8], that I will attempt an elucidation of these little known phenomena.

---

[7] See many examples in the *Annales des sciences psychiques* (Annals of the Psychic Sciences) directed by Dr. Dariex, and in general in all the spiritualist periodicals.
[8] See his latest articles in the Berlin *Sphinx* Review, and his *Philosophie der Mystik*.

To establish this theory let us start from this axiom of common sense that clairvoyance is a perception.

But what is a perception?

A perception is a sensation brought to consciousness; as nothing exists for us if we are not conscious of it, these two terms, sensation and perception, are equivalent in reality.

According to Vyasa (Patanjali commentary), sensation is that manifestation of intelligence, of the mind, which consists mainly in the recognition of the specific qualities of objects, that is to say of their phenomenal appearances.

According to Kapila[9], sensation is that mental manifestation that occurs as an appearance of what it is en rapport with.

The sensation, as we have seen, has the effect of perception.

Finally the Nyaya defines perception as the act of knowledge by which the sensory organ comes into connection with or in contact with its object[10].

---

[9] *Sankhya Yoga*, 1, an excellent summary made by Rama Prasad in 1884 in the *Theosophist*. We have borrowed a great deal from Eastern philosophy because its masters have always been unanimous in recognizing the unreality of the phenomenal world, a conclusion to which Westerners have only just arrived.

[10] R. Dubois and J. Renaut have established that the phenomenon of vision is reduced ultimately to a genuinely tactile phenomenon. In the mollusks studied by R. Dubois as in the invertebrates (Darwin), the passage from darkness to light, the luminous intensity and wavelength, the duration of the luminous excitation cause contractions of some species even though no rudiment of the eye exists. The photodermatic functions appear to us as the oldest of the sense of vision. Under the influence of luminescent rays, the skin of these invertebrates already acts as an elementary retina, and, by

These three definitions given by three different systems offer a remarkable concordance.

They indicate that the act of sensation as that of perception requires three factors to be realized:

1. That which perceives (the mind, the inner sense).
2. That which is perceived (the object in its qualities of appearance).
3. The means of perception (the sensory organ).

This is the process of knowledge described by Kapila (Aphorisms)[11], and it consists of:

1. The idea that forms the object of knowledge: Grihitri (the subjective).
2. The known: Grahana (the instrumental).
3. The act of knowledge: Grahya.

If this is the case for sensory perceptions, it must be the same for the hyperphysical perceptions, of which clairvoyance ranks first and foremost.

For this we refer to the many testimonies of experience contained in the works of modern magnetizers.

In examining the cases of clairvoyance, we will notice with M. Mohini[12] that a somnambulist subject who perceives very well

---

propagating through the superficial teguments, light determines reflex contractions analogous to those of the iris.
(J. Soury, *La Vision mentale*, Revue philos., January 95. - R. Dubois, *Le mécanisme des fonctions photodermatiques et photogéniques dans le siphon du Phola Dactylus*).
[11] We prefer Sankhya philosophy because of its deeply naturalistic character which makes it more accessible to our modern intellect.

the persons with whom his magnetizer puts him in connection with, and the places where he sends them is absolutely incapable of hearing what these people say; and vice versa, if said subject is developed in clairaudience he will not be clairvoyant; the same remark extends to psychometric manifestations.

It may be inferred from this that if in a magnetized subject the mind manifests itself sometimes by means of such hyperphysical sense, sometimes by means of another, each of these senses has a special organ. Therefore, as there is an eye, a physical ear, the astral eye, the astral ear, etc., also exist.

But if the astral senses exist, why are their manifestations so rare, and so difficult to attain? It is because we are not aware of their activities; the field of consciousness has not yet developed up to the astral plane (transcendent consciousness of the Germans).

The whole secret of the development of clairvoyance is thus solved in only this way: expanding the field of consciousness.

Let us try to define exactly this word of consciousness, so that we can find a way to develop it more quickly.

Consciousness is that faculty of the Self which makes it recognize its individualistic distinction from other objects. It is the relation that is established between the self and the non-self by means of the various systems of sensibility.

Its exercise necessarily supposes that of the faculty of perception.

---

[12] Transaction of the London Lodge of the Theosophical Society

Now the experience of each day has taught us that we perceive an object only as much as we give it our attention[13]. On the other hand, all philosophies recognize that attention is an essentially voluntary phenomenon[14]. Going back to the chain of deductions that has just been established, it can be concluded that the only way to extend the field of consciousness in view of the development of clairvoyance is the implementation of the will or desire.

How, in this case, should we use the will? Let us call here for the help of Eastern science; we will accept its teachings *a priori*, even if it is necessary to verify them by painstaking experiments.

The ancient sages of India thought that mind and matter are not opposite things, but two poles of the same light; one of the consequences of this theory led them to cloth the emotions and the ideas of the human being with a certain character of materiality.

Above the visible physical body moves the subtle body, formed of pure elements, and including all the mental apparatus (sense, intellect, consciousness).

It is in turn animated by the causal body, the first reflection of the Atman, the Divine Self, the Logos.

The subtle body comprises the five physical senses, the five psychic forces that move the five outer organs, and the five mediums through which these five driving forces operate.

---

[13] Attention: from *tendere ad,* application of the mind to an object.
[14] Ad. Franck. *Dict. Des sciences philosophiques,* p. 121.

On the other hand, the physical body is animated by certain organs which modern science calls plexus and which the Hindus call *Chakrams* or wheels; they count seven of these foci of energy in the human body:

Muladhara Chakra – sacral plexus

Swadhisthana Chakra – prostate plexus

Manipuraka Chakra – solar plexus

Anahata Chakra – cardiac plexus

Viandha Chakra – pharyngeal plexus

Ajna Chakra – cavernous plexus[15]

Sahasrara Chakra – pineal gland (the hole of Brahman)

This last foyer is the point where the physical energies sublimate to provide nourishment for the activities of the subtle body; it is therefore the point of departure and the point of arrival of the great animating current of the physical body which Sankaracharya calls Kundalini, and as such belongs to the subtle body where the mind and the consciousness are seated.

On the other hand, the sense of psychic sight[16] is localized in the cavernous plexus; in order to bring to consciousness the impressions of this organ, it suffices to speak, like the Upanishads, of passing Kundalini through the Ajna Chakra,

---

[15] *Chandilly Upanishad*, published in English by Tookaram Tatya, Bombay, 1893

[16] This organ is called by the Hindu books light of the head, eye of wisdom, celestial eye, eye of Shiva; it is the reservoir of light (Tejas), the fire that animates all men (Vaisevanara).

that is to say, in the common tongue, to concentrate by a voluntary act all the nervous force of the body in the middle of the eyebrows, the point where is the seat of the mental vision (the eye of Shiva); we will arrive there all the better if we have more nervous force in availability, by abolishing all other perception[17].

"The Yogi, says Patanjali[18], sees things by Pratibha, that is to say, by the light or knowledge instantly produced by the conjunction of the soul and the spirit, before the exercise of any reasoning faculty."

This is what we will study in the following paragraphs.

III.   <u>The Mirror</u>

The method previously given to develop the psychic senses is therefore rather difficult to follow. First of all, it requires constant surveillance of the astral organism, the sensitivity of which becomes extreme as soon as the will is directed towards the Invisible; we must then be very consistent. It is, in short, a new life which must be led, a new direction which must be printed in the mind as in the unconscious.

In this perpetual struggle with the distractions of ordinary life and with the canvas of the physical world, the will must find auxiliaries in each of the three organisms that the human

---

[17] Note also that the sense of sight summarizes and contains all the others. Refer to: *Man, Fragments of forgotten history, 1885*

[18] *Yoga Sastra*, book III. Also refer to the complementary details in the *Nyaya Siddhanta*, the *Sanhagya-Lakshmi, Dhyana-Bindou, Amrita-Bindou*, and *Tripura Upanishads*.

being understands. The intellectual man will have to put into play his faculty of meditation, by which he will consciously generate ideas; the Animated[19] Man will develop by suppressing personal emotions and gaining the power to feel the emotions of the Universal; the physical Man finally will have to close the door to the external sensations, by self-hypnosis.

All this will appear unscientific to Western readers. It is none the less true that such are the strict rules of occult education followed since the most remote times of which we can acquire the notion[20].

In fact, the beginner must, to perceive the Invisible, be isolated from the Visible. It is only later, after a long practice, patient and continued with persevering ardor, which leads to the mastery that he can be both a spectator of the occult world and the material world.

To isolate oneself from the visible is to lose consciousness; it is sleep of this kind of physical sleep, of which our modern scholars have rediscovered the most rudimentary varieties under the name of hypnotism.

Among the senses by means of which we are in relation with the visible, two are, by the materiality of their object, absolutely under the control of the will. In order to not engage the tactile and taste senses, it is sufficient to remain motionless. Forgive me for the naivety of these remarks. They are useful, if only for showing the simplicity of the

---

[19] A.B.: in French "animique", pertaining to the soul, animated, soulful
[20] We can also find evidence of this antiquity in written documents, by means of astronomy, as do the current Hindu scholars.

means used by the occult for results that are "supernatural" according to the common people.

As for the other three senses, they can be nullified by enclosing them, like the Yogis, in the silence and darkness of an underground retreat.

But then what happens is that the will is reduced to drawing its strength exclusively from the Invisible, from the astral, by means of an intellectual concentration whose power is well above the power of the majority of students, even the advanced ones.

The ideal, then, would be to furnish to the brain by the means of the three senses mentioned above an adjuvant whose uniformity and persistence would bring no distractions to the intellect. Thus the physical sense will be asleep, and the will will find new forces to practice.

The use of these adjuvants is known from the earliest antiquity. These are perfumes, music and light. The Egyptian and Hindu initiates used them as a consummated science for the development of their neophytes, and the tradition of these practices is found among all peoples. To give more details would be beyond my subject; excellent views, adapted to the modern intellect, will be found in the *Treatise on Practical Magic* by Papus[21].

Simply note this, according to the temperament of the subject[22], the ancient sages used to bring one of his senses to the magical sleep. He was then prepared by the monotonous

---

[21] Chapter V. Handling Stimulants
[22] See section 5

weakening of the other senses which I have indicated above, to a move vivid impression of the desired sense, establishing "hypnosis".

It is thus that whoever wishes to develop in clairvoyance, will at first dampen his sense of smell by an appropriate fumigation, his ear, by music of a special character, while in the semi-darkness of a small lamp he will fix his eyes on the magic mirror.

These long explanations lead one to look at the magic mirror as an instrument intended to absorb, to extract from the subject's eyes all the physical light.

But this is only the first half of its action.

We have seen how difficult and long the development of clairvoyance is when one cannot connect the latent sensitivity of Shiva's eye to the astral medium in space. It seems that if one could focus this astral light into a focal point, just as the concave mirrors do for the physical light, then clairvoyance would be much faster. Such a condition is achieved by magic mirrors. Indeed, wherever there is a concentration of physical light, there is an ethereal focus, a vibrating node of the generative medium. For spherical mirrors the problem is solved; place the subject's eye in relation to the astral focus, and at the end of a more or less considerable time, according to the degree of mental concentration or desire, that is to say, according to the perfection with which the seventh astral force of our body will have penetrated the Flaming Wheel, according to these conditions, I say (which depend directly, I repeat, on the power of the will) clairvoyance will occur. At first it will not be perfect or even precise, but a continuous and careful exercise will gradually give the astral organs all the sensitivity they are capable of acquiring.

Thus, the spherical mirrors, that is to say formed of a portion of sphere, are the most powerful. Flat disks only have the property of absorption. That's why magic discs are always saturnine in color[23].

This is the simplest explanation that one can give on the effects of the magic mirror. Let's summarize it in a few words. Given a latent faculty of discerning the astral light, to arrive at this result two opposite actions will constitute the ternary of this operation:

Use of the mirror for a dual purpose

(0)

1	2
Absorption of physical light	Concentration of a parcel of hyperphysical light in one point of space
(- -)	(- | -)

Result: Clairvoyance

I hope that the rest of these pages will undoubtedly clear up the obscurity of these explanations, and the desire of the reader will do the rest.

---

[23] See section 6

Chapter II: Realization

IV.   The Astral Kingdoms

Let us try to delve deeper into the mysteries of this universal organizing soul that we have previously identified; let us try, guided by the analogy and by the story of the seers, to describe the innumerable cells which compose it, its spheres, its powers, its hierarchies, an enormous task, and which I only tackle with my apologies. Analogously, we can first write that the Invisible is formed, like the visible, of environments and individualities, one like the other, can be divided into three large planes: the terrestrial, the lunar and the solar[24].

As for the environment, we find in each of these three planes forces analogous to those acting in man: attraction, repulsion, projection, generation, reception, adaptation and synthesis.

Realizing what they contain requires a triple training for which few men have a powerful enough mentality.

To immerse oneself in the formidable currents of these cosmic channels, it is absolutely necessary to have a perfect knowledge of their cycles, their laws and their qualities. This is not the place to make that presentation.

Considered from the point of view of individuals[25], the three planes of the Invisible can be generally attributed to the

---

[24] Refer to Alex. Saint-Yves *Les Chefs de l'Orient, La naissance* and Papus: *l'Etat de trouble* 1894

[25] A deeper analysis shows the environment in turn formed by the union of immensely numerous individuals, such as atoms. But this

elements, elementals and angels. Of these three categories of beings, those with whom our contemporaries believe to be most easily to enter in contact with are the elementals, the souls of the dead. This is true, however, only for a very small part of the Spiritist phenomena. The souls of the dead are sometimes bound to the earth by an unfulfilled desire; it is up to their pious children to shorten these torments. The ancestors come willingly, in the holy circle of the family home, when their descendants invoke them with love; they are also visible in the magic cup; but a vain curiosity should never dare to disturb their repose.

Among the elementals, some whose energies were, in the course of their earthly life, exclusively devoted to selfish ends, fall into the cursed orbs of the dark satellite. There preside the vampires, black magicians, inversive friars, doomed to the nameless sufferings of total disintegration. There is realized the law of death in its most absolute sense.

Let us divert the eyes of the seer from these places of horror, and let them penetrate into the realms of terrestrial vitality, among the elementals. Here we are with the spirits of the elements, the *Saganes* of Paracelsus. Their number defies calculation; all being, says Kabbalah, every herb, every stone has its spirit. These are the manifestations, the plastique

---

division denotes less the habits of the Western mind; I therefore thought it my duty to maintain it.
This ternary classification has been known and developed from time immemorial by the Hindus. Their 7 Lokas (places) are described by the Aryan adepts; but, wanting to give only brief indications, I confine myself to the current notions of Western tradition.

[26]powers, the innumerable armies of Nature: the *Shadaim*. Here are sad, dull greyish eyes lying in the dreary bosom of ponds and swamps; here, playing on the iridescent crest of the waves are the newts, the mermaids, and the capricious undines; sometimes friends of man, more often they are dangerous fascinators, marvelous forms of passions, the attraction of which throws man upon the pitfalls of crime and madness.

Do you hear in the underground caverns the crystalline hammers of gnomes and malicious goblins? In the depths of the invisible forges, the pygmies enclose pure souls in the shining tomb of gems; while above them, half aerial, half terrestrial, the Trolls, Nixies, and Brownies, familiar to the superstitious Welsh, play at the threshold of the cottage.

But, the seer admires the aerial forms of the fairies descending into this moonbeam; the sweetest figures of art alone can be compared to the graceful sylphs which are suitable to humans for the sweet delight of their lips; the entire Middle Ages, overcome by the terrors of dark Christian mysticism, raised its heart to her hungry for smiles. While the dreamers who live in the Black Forest –frightened by their caprice and their perfidious females – venerate the air elves with a little anxiety.

The highest of the cosmic elementals, the igneous subjects of King Jehuel and his seven ministers live in the subtle spheres of fire. The salamanders are terrible, and close to the angels, their life is long and their mores pure.

---

[26] A.B.: the term "plastique" in French can refer to flexibility, malleability, and beauty. I don't think "plastic" has retained the same connotations in English.

These four classes of beings correspond to the three kingdoms of visible nature; they are the invisible factors; a hierarchy with infinite degrees links them to each other; according to Paracelsus, the saganes are born, live, marry and die[27]; but after the time of their earthly existence, they do not retain consciousness; This is why tradition sees them as mortal[28]. Consciousness, and therefore immortality, becomes possible only when the divine animating spark has arrived at the human kingdom.

In general we are invisible to the elementals, as they are to us; they always answer our call, but the eye of flesh can perceive them only if they find in the external environment a sufficient plasticity to clothe it.

They then become for the one who evoked them, either protectors or obsessors[29].

---

[27] See *Le Comte de Gabalis*

[28] That is why he aspires, especially those of the lower realms, to draw closer to man. See the same book.

[29] In India, low caste sorcerers call them mothers, sisters or wives. See H.S. Olcott's notes in his translation of *Posthumous Humanity* by Assier; Many examples of this are found among the Redskins.
Finally, I will add a few words to this pneumatology; the studious reader may derive some benefit from the hieroglyphic analysis of the names which follow.
Kabbalah calls the male elementals *Rouchin*, and the females *Lilin*.
The spirits of Fire are ruled by Jehuel and seven ministers; those of the Water, by Michel and seven ministers; those of Earth and Water have prince Asmodee; Ruchiel and three ministers govern the spirits of the winds; Gabriel those of thunder; Nariel those of hail; the gnomes of the rocks obey Maktuniel; those of fruit trees by Alpiel, and those of other trees by Sarael; Mesannabel is the king of the spirits of the worms; Hariel and three ministers govern those of cattle. The

But on this night of the rising moon, let us send the clairvoyant beyond the sub-human spheres of life; let us place him in observation in the waves of the subterranean ether, in this ocean of force which vitalizes our planet. His dazzled eyes will be filled with ecstasy at the glory of these unknown regions; he will see, among the souls of the just, floating on the harmonious waves of the cosmic symphony, the Elohim, the secondary suns moving; he will perceive in the midst of the gigantic waves of the earth spiral the planetary spirits blessing the spirits of the peoples with their beneficent influences, while, according to the double hermetic currents, the souls descend and ascend without end, on the waves of the Celestial Fire.

But for these sublime spectacles, you need pure spectators; it requires a soul without stain and an invincible will; there we touch the sacred mysteries of ecstasy. As for such research, we do not advise undertaking it before years and years of incessant work[30]. A very ample field is already offered for the student's exploration if he knows how to limit himself to the field of physical clairvoyance, and to the study of the most external astral realms.

These are some of the most current data from the Western tradition on the beings of the astral; we are going to show the reader another aspect of the same subject by outlining a brief

---

creatures of the earth and the wave live under the control of Samniel; and the birds under that of Anpiel.

[30] To achieve them, instruments and special rites are necessary, of which we are not allowed to speak here.

compilation of the Hindu theories about it contained in the Vedas and Puranas[31].

According to the *Rig Veda* (IX, XVI, 20), there are five orders of created things; they are the Gods, Man, the Gandharvas, the Serpents and the Pitris (spirits, ancestors)[32]. These are the beings of the third and last class that we have in mind particularly.

We know that one of the fundamental theories of Vedantism teaches that Prakriti (the primordial matter), differentiated, has three qualities (the Gunas)[33]. The first is called Light (Sattva) distinguished from inertia, it is illuminating and makes things manifest; the second is called Passion (Radjo-Guna), it causes attraction and movement; the third is darkness (Tamas), it is inert, obscure, compressive.

All beings possess these three qualities to varying degrees, and it is their distinction which has served to differentiate the various classes of invisible beings; Isvara Krishna has eight[34], Sankhya-Karika (LIII), which he qualifies with the Bhagavad Gita (IX, 25 and XVII, 4), and Manu (XVII, 44, 47, 49, 50), as indicated by following table that one will like to read as well as a table of Pythagoras.

---

[31] We have borrowed extensively from the scholarly booklet *Bhutas, Pretas, and Pis'achas* by R. Ananthakrishna Shastry, Madras, 1895.
[32] The Vishnu-Purana (book 1, ch. V) gives a description of this quinary.
[33] Devi Bhagavata, III, VIII, 4. Refer to the Bhagavad Gita, XIV, 6, 7, 8, and Isvara Krishna for the definitions.
[34] Listed by his commentator Gaudapada. Amara Sinha develops this classification in Namalinganusasane, I, XI.

Gunas	Sattva	Radjas	Tamas
Sattva	Brahma Pradjapati Viradj	Devas Soma (Pitris)	Visible Creatures
Radjas	Gandharvas Yakshas	Visible Creatures	Id.
Tamas	Rakshasas Pisachas	Id.	Id.

Here are, according to more modern authorities, what are the different orders of existence around us:

a) Rupas-Devas: planetary spirits in relation with the Rupa-Loka. They are formal.

b) Arupas-Devas: the highest planetary spirits, directing the Arupa-Loka, they are formless and purely subjective.

c) Pisachas: shells that subsist in the Kama-Loka after the passage of the Ego in Devachan[35].

d) Mara-Rupas: shells with abnormal material attractions, whose spiritual and psychic life is completely null, they cannot be lead to Devachan.

e) Assuras: elementals in human form.

f) Beasts: elementals of the last rank, belonging to the various classes of animals or natural forces. These beings will develop later, along with the preceding, up to the human level.

g) Rakshasas: (demons) souls or astral forms of sorcerers, of men who have reached the limits of

---

[35] Pisachas comes from *"Pisata"* flesh, and *"as"* to eat; they are evil entities; the Pretas (disembodied souls) are similar to them and the Bhutas; but they stop their obsessions as soon as their desires have been met.

forbidden knowledge. Dead or alive, they have violated Nature.

These different names simply designate the states of existence (*Karika*, XLVIII) of the divine spark that evolves through the four astral realms, the three physical kingdoms to conquer with humanity the terrible and precious gift of its free will; above him rise the luminous realms of the Devas, below him are those of the children of Shiva[36].

These astral beings have bodies, but not conditioned by Karma[37], more or less luminous, more or less beautiful or ugly according to their spirituality; they can, moreover, perfect themselves by contemplating Brahman (*Chandogya Upanishad*, VIII, vii, 3).

All these invisible have the power of possession; beneficial in the superiors, evil in others; one can escape their hold or make them favorable by honoring them.

Those of the first class are honored by contemplating Atman; those of the second by the extinction of desires; those of the

---

[36] Shiva is the creator of the spirits of the shadow (Kalki Purana XXXI, 88); these spirits form 26 circles, mostly feminine, and which comprise three great divisions:
  1. The Balagrahas, makers of childhood diseases; their leader is Subramaniah, the youngest son of Shiva.
  2. Pramathadi Ganas, who oppose good resolutions and beneficial enterprises; their leader is Shiva's eldest son, Vinayaka.
  3. Matrikas and Baghinis, female elementals, the ugliest of all, ruled by Parvati, Shiva's wife.

It is these classes of spirits who preside over corpses (*Kalica Purana*, ch. 49), the works of the dead, etc. (*Bhagavata*, X. ch. 63)
[37] Vyasa, *Vedanta Sutra*, I, iii, 26-43

third through action; the Gandharvas are sensitive to music, perfumes and flowers; the Yakschas procure temporal goods; the Rakschasas feed on the vapor of blood shed by warlike fury; they are dispersed by Mantrams; finally, we get rid of the elementals by offering them rice balls, fulfilling their desire or by the rites of black magic[38].

V.   <u>The Seers</u>

When one proposes to begin experiments of this kind, it is not enough to know a general theory; we must also adapt to the particular case that is in sight. That is why, after having explained the mechanism of clairvoyance, we will summarize in a few lines the modifications that must be made to the general training process, according to the person to whom it is applied.

Not everyone is equally capable of clairvoyance: there are variations of environment (life, habitat, etc.), birth and habits.

Astrologically, the erection of the horoscope makes it possible to establish the temperament of the subject in a precise way to indicate to what degree the psychic senses are developable in him. We will search for these characters in the influences of the higher planets, Uranus and Neptune, which assert themselves only in exceptional cases and in individuals far in advance of the rest of the present race.

"When Neptune is powerful, its aspects with the Sun and the Moon would greatly tend to produce clairvoyance. Neptune

---

[38] *Shad Karma Dipika*

should be considered as active in the advancement of the present state of humanity only when it is near the point of the houses I, X, VII and IV, that is to say when it is angular, and its influx is consequently powerful.[39]"

Similarly, "Raphael claims to have observed that the quadratures and oppositions of Uranus with Saturn tend to produce clairvoyance[40]."

There are still many other positions of planets inclining the subject towards the hatching of these faculties; they will be found in the two excellent modern[41] treatises on astrology already cited.

But it is not always possible to resort to the erection of the natal chart (a detailed and long operation) especially when a quick experiment must be done. In this case, we can use the theory of four temperaments to classify the subject[42]; it is not a dry analytic system, it is a living and fruitful adaptation of the Great Arcana of the Word to the forms of the human figure: it gives wonderful results to the intuitive diviners.

Recently updated, this method is continued from the masters. Eliphas Levi has classified, in one of his books, the magical faculties of these four temperaments: the Melancholic is predisposed to clairaudience and geomancy; the Choleric can easily evoke or determine forms; the Sanguine is rather

---

[39] Selva. *Traité d'astrologie généthliaque*. See also the work by Abel Haatan, *Astrologie judiciaire*. 1895
[40] Guide to Astrology
[41] A.B.: They were modern in 1907
[42] Refer to the brochure with this name by Polti and Gary.

developable in psychometry; and the Phlegmatic is clairvoyant[43].

In the course of our experiments we have noticed that the subjects most naturally disposed to the development of magical faculties have eyes and hair of different colors.

Finally, the last and important recommendation: always remember that our activities generate in the Invisible forms in our image: beautiful if they are noble, ugly if they are selfish; the horrible forms usually seen at the beginning of the experiments are but the symbolic image of the ugliness of the soul, which should have been discarded at first.

VI.   <u>Classification of Mirrors</u>

Going back through the ages, the oldest written document we found on the magic mirrors are the indications from Moses' about the Urim and Thumim. This assertion may seem hazardous at first, as one recalls the disagreement of the commentators on this subject. Philo the Jew saw in it the image of the four symbolic animals[44]; others identified them

---

[43] Let us note, so as not to confuse the students, that the nomenclature of Eliphas Levi does not correspond to the terms of Polti and Gary: a little practice will quickly see the reason.

[44] See Gaffarel's *Curiosités inouyes*

"He therefore says (Philo the Jew), speaking of the history hidden in the aforementioned chapter of the Judges, that Nichas made of gold and silver three figures of young boys and three young calves, as a lion, an eagle, a dragon and a dove : so that if anyone would come to know some secret about his wife, he would question the dove; if it

with the twelve stones of the ephod, or like Eliphas Levi with the two onyx placed as clips on the shoulders of the high priest[45]. It has been believed to recognize the incommunicable name, the names of the twelve tribes: however, the mere examination of the biblical text shows that none of these explanations fully satisfies.

Here, however, is the revelation we find in *Art Magic*, presented in the crystal by a planetary genius.

"The best and oldest method of divination is that of the Crystal or the Urim and the Thummim.

Its origin was heavenly, and the inspirations, visions, and communications received by means of crystal by a holy and pure man, were purely divine and free from all human influence. The use of crystal in modern times is almost as powerful as the Urim and the Thummim of the Jews. And in the hands of a clairvoyant subject, his revelations are infallible.

Spirits do not actually appear in the crystal, but the seer receives a magnetic aid to penetrate the spiritual world deeply through the translucence of the instrument, by this way he (or she) is brought to a very intimate contact with spirits who can willingly converse with mortals."

The hieroglyphic analysis of the Hebrew words confirms this view. Thummim's root is T M, "the sign of signs, the symbol

---

regarded his children, then the young boy; if for riches, then the eagle; if for strength and power, then the lion; if for fertility, then the horse or calf; if for the length of days and years, then the dragon." (Quote by Eliphas Levi)

[45] *Rituel*, p. 336

of all perfection, the accomplished image of the universal soul". On the other hand, the plural I M means universal passive manifestation: the general idea is therefore that of reflection, of image received and rendered faithfully, of shimmering water, the magic crystal.

On the other side, Aourim is the general manifestation of light, meaning that, materialized, leads to that of reflecting mirror.

In any case, I will not insist further, not wishing to impose an opinion.

In India, at the present, the Chelas, "initiated students", use gold mirrors in the crypts of the temples.

Historical antiquity has seen a great variety of metallic mirrors, used for both black magic and white.

"The Sagas of Thessaly once traced on their mirrors their sibylline formulas with blood. As soon as the moon (another mirror) reflected these bloody characters, then the answer was printed on its silver crescent. This is how the oracle was rendered.[46]"

In Japan, the mirrors are very large, in jade or any other stone of a perfect polish. You can see some very beautiful specimens at the Guimet Museum.

Papus described in a lecture made to the Independent Group of Esoteric Studies, a magic mirror brought from India by the painter James Tissot. It consists essentially of an bright crystal sphere on which the subject fixes his eyes.

---

[46] Stanislas de Guaita, *Temple de Satan*, p. 367

The magicians of the Middle Ages used mainly metallic mirrors, tin or copper. The crystal of St. Helena was also used by them; we will give its consecration later. The famous Nostradamus was not an astrologer but rather a seer; all his prophecies were presented to him in the mirror. One of the most eminent occultists of the Renaissance, Dr. John Dee received from spirits a very precious magical stone[47]. The manuscripts preserved in the Cottonian library speak of it as a crystal; other authors represent it as a piece of circular coal, perfectly polished, provided with a handle[48]. In 1842 it was with Horace Walpole in Strawberry Hill. It was sold for 336 francs to an unknown purchaser[49].

Among the black mirrors, we can cite the Arabic Mandeb, whose process we shall see later; the mirror of du Potet[50], a circle drawn and blackened with charcoal on the floor[51]; among those invented by the students of this powerful magnetizer, here is one of the best: a piece of oval cardboard, about ten centimeters long, covered on one side with tin foil, on the other with a piece of cloth. The operator strongly magnetises this mirror, and when he finds the occasion," he

---

[47] Refer to the excellent article *Vie de Jean Dee*, published in L'Initiation (December 93 to April 94) by our late brother Albert Poisson.

[48] A.B. :remember this was written in 1907, today we know the mirror was obsidian

[49] Art Magic

[50] A.B.: Jules Denis, Baron du Potet (1796-1881) was a French esotericist, mesmerist, and Doctor of Homeopathy.

[51] Edmond Bourdain published (Paix Universelle 1895 and Progrès spirite) the account of spiritual experiences realized with the mirror of du Potet. The spirits evoked made appear in the blackened circle the answers to the questions asked.
See also evocations of the dead, made in India, in bottles filled with ink. Theosophist, August 1882, March 1883, December 1884.

takes it in his right hand; pressed against the palm of his hand, his fingers surrounding the edges like so many magnetic points through which the fluid escapes, he presents this mirror on one side or the other, about a foot away from the root of the nose; ten minutes of fixation is sufficient to obtain vision, if it is to take place[52]."

<u>The Swedenborg Mirror</u>

Cahagnet describes this mirror in *les Arcanes de la vie future* and in *Magie magnétique*. It was revealed by a spirit that presented itself as the illustrious Swedish seet, to the somnambulist Cahagnet.

Here is how you can build one:

"We take any quantity of graphite, sifted very fine, which is stirred (in a suitable vase that can be placed in a fire), with a sufficient quantity of olive oil so as to form a fairly clear paste; place this mixture over a low heat to better facilitate the mixing; we take an ordinary looking-glass (without tinning) that we gently approach the fire to prepare it to receive the mixture without experiencing a transition that can make it break; place it flat on two pieces of wood and then the prepared paste is poured on one of its faces, by turning it from one side to the other side in order to give the liquid the facility to cover equally all the parts, this is better than to use a brush which would leave furrows that would ruin the uniformity. If the paste is a little light, sprinkle the same sifted

---

[52] Cahagnet, *Magie magnétique*, p. 82

graphite over all of it, which would make a more compact amalgam.

This mirror thus prepared is laid flat horizontally on a piece of furniture and cannot be used until a few days later, having been placed in a suitable frame for this purpose. This mirror has the advantage, over tinned ones, of tiring the sight less by not rendering a perfect image of objects; it is good to place it in a place so that it does not reflect the image of the person who wants to fixate on it. I am using this mirror like all of those I have spoken of, standing behind the consultant, magnetically fixing it to the cerebellum (above the dimple of the neck) with the intention that the fluid that I project on him by my eyes joins with his to illuminate it. I also mentally pray to the angel committed to guarding this person, to facilitate this vision if he finds it suitable. I obtained with this mirror the same results as with the others.[53]"

The 1894 *Almanach du Magiste* (*Magician's Almanac*) recounts experiences with a mirror made of a slightly charred wood disk. Here is how the experimenter accounts for his visions:

"After a few minutes of fixity, the surface of the mirror is veiled and covered with a slight whitish vapor. Gradually, this vapor increases and is transformed into a kind of bluish and phosphorescent light. It spreads even on surrounding objects, to which it communicates a particular brilliance. In the end, it rolls in big clouds that quickly traverse the field of the mirror.

---

[53] Magie magnétique, p. 83 - Cahagnet has also reissued the metal mirrors of antiquity under the name of galvanic mirrors, composed of copper and zinc, carefully burnished. This device is very powerful; its magnetism is positive, electric.

It is only then that the forms are shown and that I sometimes distinguish very clearly what I want to see."

Among the luminous mirrors we note the mirror of Cagliostro, the mirror of St. Helena, the crystal or magnetic mirror, the narcotic mirror whose water is obtained by the distillation of magic plants, etc. etc.[54]

"In a carafe full of clear water or a magnetized crystal ball; it is in such environments, very refractive for the astral light, that Cagliostro had his *colombes* focus their gaze upon for a long time. He appointed young boys who were still innocent or little girls who played the role of passive clairvoyants, while he was holding them under the irradiation of his magnetic will. These little beings saw then the chain of the future contingents, in the form of a series of evidently sibylline images, concrete kinds of prophecies, which only awaited their translation into demotic[55] language. The colombes spoke in exclamations. Suddenly Cagliostro in an inspired and vibrant voice, improvised an oratorical or dithyrambic[56] commentary, and the most mocking souls and the most skeptical minds were then subjugated.[57]"

Finally, the Comte de Gabalis gives the recipe for four kinds of mystical containers to attract the spirits of the elements.

---

[54] In Ragon's, *Maçonnerie occulte*, we will find details of the magnetic disks that an intelligent experimenter can easily use for lucidity experiments.

[55] A.B.: demotic – denoting or relating to the kind of language used by ordinary people

[56] A.B.: dithyramb – a wild choral hymn of ancient Greece, especially one dedicated to Dionysus; a passionate or inflated speech, poem, or other writing.

[57] Stanislas de Guaita, *Le Temple de Satan*, p. 342

To attract Salamanders, take glass globes filled with "feu du monde" (world fire) concentrated over forty days; to attract the sylphs, other spheres filled with conglobated air; for the undines, these vases will be filled with water, and with salted earth for the Gnomes. We entrust to the reader's insight the task of discovering the real meaning of this recipe.

We can see that the mirrors can be classified as follows:

Saturnian mirrors[58] - discs and instruments of black color

Lunar mirrors – vases and crystals filled with water

Solar mirrors – portions of metallic spheres

The first are better suited to young boys, the second to women; the last are rather synthetic, and are addressed to the seers without a director.

Each of these large classes can in turn be divided into four genera, appropriate to the various temperaments of those who are called upon to use them. One can vary the composition, adapting them to the four Zodiacal temperaments, or the seven planets. This is easy to do when one is a little versed in the theory of correspondences.

These are the main varieties of magic mirrors. Through experimentation many more can be found; we will leave to the researchers the pleasure of these discoveries.

---

[58] We intentionally left out all the theory studying the size of the mirror, its curvature, its handling, waiting for more complete experiences.

Chapter III: Adaptation

VII. The Practice

The fundamental rule of all occult experience - and those of which we are speaking here, possess this character in the highest degree - is to never use any object before having consecrated it, to never begin anything without an invocation to the invisible.

Thus, any attempt at clairvoyance must be preceded by a consecration of the instrument. We will list and describe some of these rites starting with the simplest.

Lucidity with the Glass of Water

Papus recommends the following procedure, applicable in a mundane salon as well as in the silence of the oratory[59]:

"The simplest magic mirror consists of a crystal cup (not glass) filled with water to the edge and placed on a table covered with a white cloth. Behind the cup, two candles are placed and everything is ready for the operation. This operation requires the assistance of two people: a subject and a director.

The subject sits in front of the cup in order to see the horizontal surface of the water.

It is then that the operator approaches and standing, places his right hand extended on the head of the subject and calls the angel who presides over this operation three times.

---

[59] *Almanach du Magiste*, p. III, and *Traité de Magie pratique*, passim

After a minute (if successful) the subject sees the water boiling: then, the colors of the specter appear, and finally visions are shown and answers to mental questions are given."

Metallic Mirror

Here is the rite of consecration used by the Western magicians of the Middle Ages as given by several manuscripts of the *Clavicules*[60].

"Take a shiny, well - polished plate of lightly concave steel, and write on it with the blood of a male, white pigeon, at the four corners of the mirror the names:

Jehovah   Elohim

Metatron   Adonai

Put the steel in new, very clean and white linen.

When you see the new moon in the first hour after the setting sun, come to a window, look at the sky with devotion, and say:

O LORD! O eternal King! Ineffable God who created all things for my sake, and by a judgment hidden for the health of man, look upon me, (Name), your very unworthy servant, and consider my intention pure. Deign to send me your angel Anael on this mirror whom summons, commands and orders his companions and your subjects that you have

---

[60] What we are going to transcribe is taken from the manuscripts of the library of Papus, and is reproduced in the Treatise on Practical Magic, p. 308 et seq.

*made, O almighty who have been, who are and who will be forever; that
in your name they pray and act righteously to instruct me and show me
what I will ask of them.*

Then, throw on burning coals the suitable perfume which is
oriental saffron and upon throwing it, say:

*In this, for this, and with this that I pour out before your face, oh my
God, who is triune, good, and in the most sublime elevation, whom sees
above the cherubim and seraphim, and whom is to judge the ages by fire,
hear me.*

At this moment, the mirror is perfumed by putting it over a
new stove of earthenware or iron so that it is impregnated
with the smoke of the perfume, holding it with your right
hand and saying the previous prayer three times.

After saying it, blow three times on the mirror and say:

*Come, Anael, come, and may it be your pleasure to be in me by your
will, in the name of the Almighty Father +, in the name of the most
wise Son +, in the name of the most gracious Holy Spirit +; come
Anael, in the name of the terrible Jehovah, come Anael by virtue of the
immortal Elohim, come Anael by the arm of the all-powerful Metatron,
come to me N... (Say your name on the mirror), and command your
subjects that with love, joy and peace, they will show to my eyes the things
that are hidden from me. So mote it be, Amen.*

After doing this, lift your eyes to the sky and say:

*Almighty Lord, who moves all that pleases you, hear my prayer and may
my desire be pleasing to you; look please, Lord, upon this mirror and
bless it, so that Anael, one of your subjects, is secured with his
companions to satisfy N ..., your poor and miserable servant, O God,*

blessed and most exalted of all the heavenly spirits, who live and reign in the eternity of good. So mote it be.

When you have done these things, make the sign of the cross on you and on the mirror, the first day and the following for forty-five consecutive days, at the end of which Anael will appear under the figure of a beautiful child, you will greet and command his companions to obey you.

Note that it does not always take forty-five days to perfect the mirror; often the spirit appears on the fourteenth day. It depends on the intention, the devotion and the fervor of the operator.

Thereafter, when you want to see in the mirror and obtain what you want, it is not necessary to recite all the aforementioned prayers; but after perfuming the mirror, say:

Come Anael, may it be your pleasure, etc…. (up to the Amen).

When the operation is over, you will dismiss the spirit by saying:

I thank you, Anael, for coming and satisfying my request; go in peace and come when I call you.

The scent or perfume of Anael is saffron.

Saturnian Mirrors

Disks and mirrors of this kind are only able to render visible inferior or bad spirits, or physical objects, there is no special consecration for them.

Mirror of Saint Helena

Make a cross on a crystal glass with olive oil, and under the cross write St. Helena. Then, give to a child, virgin, born of the legitimate marriage the crystal glass to hold, kneel behind him, and say the following prayer three times:

Deprecor, Domina Helena, mater regis Constantini, etc.

When the child will see the angel; he will be able to make such a request to him as one wishes[61].

Nostradamus Formula

Frequently used successfully in evocations of planetary or other spirits by nineteenth century adepts, this rite is one of the highest and purest of its genre. Only the secret rite of the Hindu Chela is superior to it[62]. Having obtained a good and clear stone, in which no spirit has yet been called, the seer will have to determine that for all uses, except for evil. I do not mean that he should propose to use it only for good use, for many frivolous and futile questions can be made, which will make the stone serve the knowledge of worldly things. But that he resolves not to use it for bad or unholy purposes; he will then dedicate it by fervent prayer to God. Do not use a mediator for this prayer, but with firmness, with humility, hope that God will put you in possession of a guardian spirit by which you will eventually obtain the desired visions.

---

[61] *Le petit Albert,* and various other grimoires.
[62] Art Magic, p. 420 and following.

Having done this, inspect the crystal, and before asking to see any vision, ask for the name of your guardian spirit; having obtained this name, ask to see the angel; when it appears, ask it to give you whatever advice it thinks fit. Ask it for the days and times it would like to appear, and also the times when you can call other spirits. Ask that it will guard your crystal well, to prevent evil spirits from appearing there, and to give you warning in time if it happens to attack you, so that you or it can defend you.

All this being agreed, give it liberty; at the first evocation, it must not be retained for more than half an hour.

When you evoke it for the second time, exorcise it three times, with a firm and determined will, before asking it any questions. If it does not vanish, you can then count on it absolutely.

You can then continue the evocations as long as it will be possible, according to your convenience and that of the angel; if it wishes to leave, it can do so without dismissal; but be careful not to forget the "dismissal" after finishing one night.

When you invoke some atmospheric or lower-level spirit, such as those of the dead, always use the formula: *If it is convenient* [63] *and pleasant to you*, or *According to your pleasure*. Do this especially when you are talking to the spirit of a living person. These words are not needed when it comes to the guardian or a high grade spirit.

---

[63] A.B.: the term convenable in French can mean – suitable, appropriate, proper, fitting, correct, etc.

Above all things, you are advised not to use this Angel for any purpose; it is not a direct or indirect way to make money. It may seem to continue its services sweetly for some time; you can get the information and visions you want; but the fatal and lamentable consequences of our ill-considered demands will come sooner or later.

When at last you are in possession of a good crystal, have confidence in it, and make sure by all means of its veracity. You can also use a mirror, which is by far the best.

The mirror is used in the same way as the crystal; but its visions are of a natural grandeur[64] and by the bay which it opens to the spiritual world, it makes it possible to be more intimately connected with the spirit to which one is addressing.

Of all the modes of divination, this one is the easiest and the best; its information is slow and crude at first, but little by little you are brought by it to the summum of all human knowledge on spiritual subjects.

The Call:

"In the name of Almighty God, in whom we live, we move and we have our being, I humbly implore the Guardian Angel of this mirror to appear."

When it comes, you can ask it your questions, and get information, such as when it will let you call it again, and for how long.

---

[64] This is a particular kind of mirror, not yet described, and we leave the discovery to the intuition of students (P.S.)

For a Vision:

"In the name of Almighty God, in whom we live, we move and we have our being, I humbly implore the spirit of this mirror to favor me with a vision which interests me and which instructs me etc ... (name the vision).

To see a Person:

"In the name of Almighty God, in whom we live, we move and we have our being, I pray to you N... *to appear in this mirror, if it is convenient and agreeable to you* (never forget these words).

Exorcism:

"In the name of Almighty God, in whom we live, we move and we have our being, I dismiss and expel the Spirit currently visible in this mirror, if it is not N ... (Name the spirit) *or if it is not a good and truthful Spirit.*

This must be pronounced in a very energetic and very stern voice, repeated three times, the forefinger on the crystal.

Dismissal Formula:

"In the name of Almighty God, in whom we live, we move and we have our being, I dismiss from this mirror all the spirits who have descended here; and may the peace of God be forever between them and me.

This must be repeated three times, before closing the session, even if the spirit does not appear.

<u>**Mandeb**</u>

The magic mirror used by the Arabs consists of a small round of thick ink that the sorcerer pours into the palm of a child's left hand; detailed accounts of visions can be found in the works of Count Laborde and W. Lane. Here is a brief description of the operation according to Léon de Laborde[65]:

First two formulas are written on two strips of paper: the first is a sentence from the Koran (chapter 50, verse 21); the other consists of the following invocation:

"Tarschoun! Tarzuschoun! Descend! Descend! Be present! Where did the prince and his army go? Where did El-amar go? The Prince and his army? appear servants of this name!"

This incantation is repeated on six pieces of paper, while the sentence of the Koran is attached to the subject's headdress; all of it is first offered to the smoke of an incense composed of equal parts of Takeh mabachi and Konsombra Diaon (incense, coriander seeds) to which Indian amber is added.

The figure of the mirror being drawn in the hand of the young object, we throw the first formula of conjuration into the fire, while intoning these words:

Anzilu aiouha el Dschemonia and Dshennoum

Anzilu betakki matalabontontron aleikum

Taricki, etc. (2 times)

---

65 Karl Kiescwetter (Sphinx, 1890) believes that the Arab magician named Abd-el-Kader-el-Moghrebi, of which Laborde speaks, is none other than the famous Emir who later became our enemy.

Anzilu, etc. (3 times)

Taricki, etc. (2 times)

The operator continues holding the subject's hand until the sweeper appears:

Note that Jean Dee and Kelley also saw at the beginning of their evocations a figure of man sweeping a place. Karl Kiesewetter[66] finds it "the symbol of the destruction of the material obstacles of clairvoyance". One might consider this as particular to a circle of initiation. In experiments of this kind undertaken in Paris for some years we have never seen or heard this symbol.

The magician of Mr. de Laborde came when the sweeper disappears seven planetary banners in the following order: Mars, Saturn, Moon, Venus, Jupiter, Mercury, and the Sun, after burning the second formula, then when the banners have vanished, the third portion is also thrown into the fire. The subject then sees arriving troops (fourth and fifth formulas) who pitch tents, kill an ox, cook it and eat it. It is then that he is ready to answer the questions of the assistants.

Mirror of the Bhattahs

Five English officers, including the narrator[67], one day attended the illuminating dance of the Muntra-Vallahs, or Brahman magicians. This rite was celebrated at Mutra (in the kingdom of Agra, on the west bank of the Djumna); this city

---

[66] Akademïsche Monaishefte
[67] Colonel Stephen Fraser

is famous for the output it makes of magical instruments; it is one of only two places in the world where the preparation of the Paraphtaline gum used for the mirror vision is known. These Brahmans call the state in which one is enlightened, the sleep of Siolam.

Some mystical writers believe that they gathered their knowledge in the "left hand path" where their neighbors the Dougpas of Bhutan would have directed them. We cannot affirm anything specific about this subject.

We will summarize Colonel Fraser's long description:

On the appointed day, our five officers went, through the gorges of the Chocki-Hills, to the village where the mysterious "Sebeiyeh" dance was to take place. The sheik, an old man more than a hundred years old, judging by the venerable air and the white beards of his grandchildren, received them with courtesy and immediately began the preparations for the ceremony.

A circle was first made on the ground by two couples of engaged young people carrying earthen vessels; a black, viscous, tar-like liquid filled these vases; the sheikh informed them that this substance, collected in the volcanic crevices of the Mahadeo Hills (Gondivana, Decan), is harvested by young boys and girls who have not yet reached the age of puberty; it can only be found during the month of June; it is then subjected to occult preparations, during forty-nine days by other young people on the eve of getting married.

This circle was made around a small altar of stones, on which the sacred fire of the Garounahs burns without ever extinguishing. A tripod supported above that fire a large earthen vessel, where the four young operators poured a quarter of the contents of their vessels; Hundreds of assistants were ranged around the circle, and some of them frantically sounded drums and large cymbals, a strange prelude to the following sacred enthusiasms.

The sheikh, meanwhile, indicated to the officers the symbol of fire, the universal soul of nature, always active; above it, however, are the three divine powers of Para Brahm: tripod ideal of creation, preservation, transformation; a pole covered with the skins of cobra snakes (remarkable coincidence) crowned with a palm nut, is sunk in the ground near the altar; it is the image of the creative power of the divinity, of the rigid, penetrating male force, while the vase subjected to the action of fire represents the passive, fundamental, enveloping power of the feminine force.

In accordance with the exciting rhythms of the supplicating voices, the bursts of the copper flutes, the sound of the drums and barbarian instruments, begins a strange dance punctuated by the piercing cries of women and girls, gradually exalted up to religious fury; while the echoes of the neighboring rocks respond to this powerful concert like the voices of the Devas favorable to the desires of mortals.

Moving forward with a voluptuous and gentle movement, to which the whole body seemed to take part, the young, supple and graceful girls, adorned with all the splendors of Oriental luxury, expressed with indescribable charm, by the inflexions of their slender bust, by light genuflections, by the rolling gestures of their arms, the most ideal poetry of love; they revolved around the phallic emblem, stirring with silver spatulas the contents of the vase they carried, while the two couples who had inaugurated the ceremony performed symmetrical rhythms.

The old Brahmin then spoke; but his voice without timbre, far from interrupting the state of contemplation in which this spectacle and this music had thrown the strangers, penetrated with a magnetic power to the heart of their minds to model them like a soft wax, in the first directions of occult practice.

He revealed to them in gemmed language the precious flowers of oriental poetry, the true nature of passion. He showed it to them as the secret root of the human soul, as the support of all existence, as the invisible spring that moves every creature; pure essence at first, then divided into the innumerable hierarchy of Forces, it is the elixir for whom conquers it, it is sacred and reveals itself as the all - powerful arm of the one who dominates it.

The substance contained in these vases, added the Sheik, is charged with passion, and it is by the magical power of the latter, when, just now, crystals will be covered with this liquid, that the seers will be able to contemplate not only any scene of earthly life but even the enchanting images of the sojourn of the Gods. Such is the true Door, concludes the Brahmin in a final whisper.

The musicians had meanwhile accelerated their rhythm and the dancers their movements, the first two couples of fiancés suddenly broke away the eldest of the girls, and while her companions began to stir the black mass suspended on the fire, uttering magnetic incantations, she left, continuing to dance, her tunic of gold to offer to the delighted eyes the royal alms of her beauty.

The perfect contours of her young bust were bathed in the luminous air of the vespers with transparencies of opal; the entanglement of her untied black hair brightened the delicacy of her breasts, the noble curves of her flanks; like the marvelous flower of some dream plant, the fine oval of her head crowned with splendor the shivering bust of the young bayadère, while the play of her languid eyelids scattered on all things the magical prestige of her eyes.

Her art was ignorant of the hasty movements of our choreography; symbols vivified by force of science from the high conceptions of the sanctuary, each of her steps revealed an Arcanum, and each of her gestures evoked a Power. Undulations of the torso, swaying of the hips accompanied the interlacing of the young arms, while the divine look of the virgin seemed to deliver her all to the beloved ideal; it was the very palpitations of the soul which we thought we saw translated into the body of an indescribable and chaste kind; the undulating waves of her voluptuous movements lent themselves to the expression of the thousand shades of desire and modesty that enraptured the silent spectators. For beauty resides only in the inexpressible mystery.

The colonel was suddenly drawn from his admiring contemplation by the hieratic dancer who invited him to take a look at the contents of the great magic vase; instead of a black and boiling mass, he saw with astonishment some of the most delicate colors, constantly changing into ever - changing forms of shimmering flowers; the high priest poured a layer of this liquid on the waters of which our hero saw friends and relatives dear to his heart, as well as several other extraordinary images

Please excuse the length of the extract that we have adapted; we wanted to put the mystical reader on the path of one of the most powerful secrets of the Eastern Temple.

Communication with a Planetary Spirit

Whenever guardian spirits, or angels of the highest order, move in the spiritual world, the air around them is purified of all that is, to some degree, less refined than themselves. Thus, when an atmospheric spirit encounters a more celestial spirit, the atmospheric spirit yields to the pressure of the area surrounding the other and withdraws to give it passage. In this way the spirits visit our atmosphere, and the spheres lower than their own, like the earth, without ever coming into contact with the individualities inferior to it, unless they desire it. Thus, even when a spirit is called to converse with human beings, the thought of the Evocateur, or rather his will, immediately reaches him, and he appears to separate and repel before him all influences less angelic than his.

The guardian spirits, and the angels of high degree, can only be seen in the Urim or the Thumim, the crystal and the mirror; the other modes of divination, by vases of water, by shadows, by blindfold, or black fluids, are effective only to see dead people, atmospheric spirits, bad or undeveloped wandering spirits[68].

....

---

[68] Art Magic, passim.

Let's quickly summarize all of this.

Man possesses latent within his being, the faculty of communicating with the Invisible. He can do it either by light or by sound, or by each of the five other organs of the astral senses that esotericism recognizes. In the first case the power he develops is clairvoyance. We have seen, with certain environments and certain beings, this faculty put him in contact, we have finally endeavored to determine what would be the instrument for each person that would offer him the most effective help in this arduous and dangerous task. This memento is very incomplete; it has many shortcomings both from a theoretical and a practical point of view. I do not present more with confidence to the special public that has interest in it; if only because it is an almost complete summary of what has been printed so far on this subject.

Sincere workers will find here the only true and solid basis for the practice of divination.

<u>Bibliography</u>

1. Art Magic: Or Mundane, Sub Mundane and Super Mundane Spiritism. 1876
2. Cahagnet. Magie magnétique ou traité historique et pratique, etc.
3. Eliphas Levi. Rituel de haute Magie. Ch. XX.
4. U.-N. Badaud. Coupd'oeil sur la Magie au XIX siècle. 1891
5. Recherches sur la magie égyptienne par Léon de Laborde. 1841
6. Papus. Traité élémentaire de magie pratique. 1893
7. Papus. Les Miroirs magiques, conférence faite au groupe indépendant d' Etudes ésotériques. (In le Voile d'Isis)
8. Carl Du Prel. Das Kreus am Ferner, roman Suttgard, Cotta. 1891 (or its analysis in L'Initiation issue of June 1892).
9. William Lane. Moeurs et coutumes des Egyptiens actuels traduit en allemande par le Dr. Julius-Theodor Zenker.
10. Gorres. Mystique divine, naturelle et diabolique, trad. De Ch. Ste-Foi
11. Casaubonus. A true and faithfull relation of what passed for many years between Dr. John Dee and some spirits. (analysis by Philophotes in L'Initiation, January-April edition 1894).
12. Lettres édifiantes et curieuses, etc.
13. De Sacy. Exposition de la religion des Druses.
14. Potter. Travels in Syria.
15. Von. Hammer. Hist. des Sasseins.
16. Youatt. Research into magic Arts.
17. Col. Fraser. Twelve Years in India.

18. Le grand et le petit Albert.
19. Agrippa: Philos. Occ.

www.ingramcontent.com/pod-product-compliance
Lightning Source LLC
Chambersburg PA
CBHW030409160726
47992CB00007B/3035